FLORENCE NIGHTINGALE

Kristi Lorene

Illustrated by
Ken Save

BARBOUR
PUBLISHING, INC.
Uhrichsville, Ohio

© MCMXCVII by Barbour Publishing, Inc.

ISBN 1-55748-104-6

Published by Barbour Publishing, Inc., P.O. Box 719, Uhrichsville, Ohio 44683
http://www.barbourbooks.com

Member of the
Evangelical Christian
Publishers Association

Printed in the United States of America.

FLORENCE NIGHTINGALE

"LET'S GO TO FLORENCE FOR THE BIRTH OF THE NEW BABY."

1
Early Years

On the terrace of their estate called Lea Hurst in the south of England, Fanny and William Nightingale sat watching their daughter, Parthe, playing in her playpen.

"William," Fanny said, resting her hand on her protruding stomach. "Let's go to Florence for the birth of the new baby."

"Excellent idea, my dear!" William exclaimed.

Florence, Italy was one of the most exciting and liveliest cities in the world. Every night there were parties and fancy balls. Fanny Nightingale adored the opera there. She was quite popular and was invited many places.

W.E.N., as William Nightingale was often called by friends and family, also loved the city of Florence, but for different reasons. He enjoyed quiet time, reading, and studying. There was much to learn in Florence, Italy.

As a rich English couple, the Nightingales travelled often. W.E.N. and his wife had inherited a great deal of money and did not need to work for a living, so they had much free time on their hands. Their first child, Parthe, had been born in Naples, Italy.

Fanny Nightingale was a romantic woman who loved unusual names. Parthe had been named Parthenope (Parthen-o-pe), the Greek name for the city of Naples, Italy, where she had been born.

On May 12, 1820, the Nightingales were again blessed with another daughter. "She will be named Florence," Fanny said, "after the city of her birth."

The family returned to England when Florence was a year old. Parthe was two.

The Nightingales had two homes. During the summer, they lived at Lea Hurst. The house, designed by William, had fifteen bedrooms. The estates had ponies, birds, dogs, and cats. Florence loved the animals and took care of them when they were sick or injured.

DURING THE SUMMER, THEY LIVED AT LEA HURST.

The Nightingales had a winter home called Embley, near London, where Mrs. Nightingale preferred to live.

"It's closer to my friends," she said to William. "You know how I love to have company." Fanny's guests at Embley often stayed for weeks.

The two Nightingale girls, who called each other Flo and Parthe, enjoyed everything their parents' money could buy. But they were very different from each other. Parthe was much like her mother. She loved having fun and riding her pony in the gardens.

"Don't you ever have any fun?" Parthe would ask Flo, who often sat reading or studying.

"This is fun," Flo replied. "I like to read and learn about new things."

Parthe rolled her eyes and trotted off.

Florence was quiet and studious, like her father. Bright, pretty, and graceful, she had large, gray eyes and reddish-brown hair.

But Florence also had a stubborn streak that sometimes

"THIS IS FUN."

made people feel awkward. Florence lived a life of extremes. People either showered her with extravagant praise, or with extravagant blame. Some people saw her as sweet and tenderhearted; others found her cold, ruthless, and quarrelsome. Parthenope was liked by more people than Florence was.

But Florence was, indeed, often a tenderhearted person. When she loved someone, she gave all of herself to them and expected the same in return. She was closest to her Aunt Mai, William Nightingale's sister.

The family was in London for Florence's seventh birthday. After cake and presents, the family went for a walk. William stopped outside Kensington Palace, the royal home.

"That's where little Princess Victoria lives," he told his youngest daughter. "Her birthday is in May, too. She's eight."

Florence felt proud to share her birth month with the future Queen of England. "I'm only one year younger

"THAT'S WHERE LITTLE PRINCESS VICTORIA LIVES."

than her!" she exclaimed.

"They say that Victoria is a little May flower."

Mr. Nightingale continued, bending to kiss his daughter's nose. "But you, Florence, are *my* little May flower."

Florence felt so happy, she skipped ahead of her parents.

"I've got a surprise for you, Florence," her mother said as they walked. "Aunt Mai is getting married, and you will be a bridesmaid."

Florence stopped dead in her tracks and burst into tears. "No!" she bawled. "I won't let her!"

Fanny and William tried to comfort their daughter. Florence loved her Aunt Mai so much, it terrified her to think she had to share her with anyone.

"Florence," her mother cooed. "Aunt Mai will love you and her husband."

But as far as Florence was concerned, her birthday was ruined by this news.

As summer passed, Florence grew to accept her Aunt Mai's impending marriage. Still, when she saw how happy

"AUNT MAI WILL LOVE YOU AND HER HUSBAND."

the bride looked on the wedding day, Florence felt she was losing the only person who had ever understood her.

Mai and her groom knelt at the altar. Florence suddenly ran up and knelt between them. Mai smiled and put her arm around Florence. "It's all right, Florence," she whispered.

Aunt Mai had married Fanny Nightingale's brother, Sam Smith. Florence was eleven when the Smith's first child was born. She often held the baby in her arms and called him, "my boy, Shore." Florence adored Shore all her life, and he returned her affections as he grew up.

During her childhood, Florence began a habit she would keep all her life. Writing. She kept a diary, scribbled thoughts on bits of paper, and used writing to work through things that were bothering her.

"Anytime I want to remember something important," she explained to Parthe, "I get an old envelope or whatever I can find." She never threw away these odd bits of paper and private notes.

Florence knew she was different from Parthe and other

FLORENCE BEGAN A HABIT SHE WOULD KEEP ALL HER LIFE.

little girls. Florence secretly feared she was a monster. Sometimes, she stood in front of her mirror to see if she looked like a monster. She felt so different from her peers.

Parthe loved her mother's tea parties, dressing up, and meeting new people. But Florence hated the parties. Meeting people made her stomach churn.

One afternoon, Mrs. Nightingale and Parthe were having tea with cousins. Mrs. Nightingale grew annoyed.

"Parthe, run upstairs and tell your sister her tea is getting cold. And soon there won't be any cake left."

"Yes, Mama."

Parthe hurried up to Flo's room, where she was "nursing" her sick dolls.

"Everyone's waiting, Flo. Mother is angry and wants you to hurry downstairs."

Florence shook her head stubbornly. "I don't want to."

"But our cousins brought their friends to meet us."

"I won't like them and they won't like me."

Parthe was bewildered by her sister's moods. Flo was

FLO WAS "NURSING" HER SICK DOLLS.

happier doing multiplication tables than at parties having tea and cakes. Parthe hated her lessons!

"Flo," Parthe continued, stamping her foot. "If you don't hurry downstairs, we'll both be in trouble."

Florence stamped her foot. "I won't leave my sick dolls! They need me to take care of them!"

"Please!" Parthe begged. "You're going to get me into trouble. I'll give you my piece of cake."

"I hate the way Mother's guests pat me on the head. And tea parties are just not useful."

"Oh, Flo, stop being so babyish and come along. Mother will be furious!"

Florence reluctantly put on her best dress and followed Parthe downstairs.

I'd rather be upstairs doing mathematics, she thought as she politely curtsied to their guests.

Florence loved learning. In those days, wealthy families like Florence's did not send their girls to school. They were taught only music and art and were expected to

"OH, FLO, STOP BEING SO BABYISH AND COME ALONG."

marry rich gentlemen and have children.

But William Nightingale thought it was important for the girls to have an education. When Florence was twelve, he began teaching them history, philosophy, and five languages, including Latin and Greek.

Fanny and William frequently disagreed over the girls' lessons. Fanny thought it all unnecessary.

"They do not need to know Latin to make good society wives."

"Nevertheless," William said, "the lessons will continue."

One summer afternoon, William read to them from an Italian book. Parthe had trouble paying attention. Her mind wandered to arranging flowers with her mother and the dinner party coming that evening. She yawned.

"How do you like the story, Parthe?" William Nightingale boomed.

Parthe's face flushed. "I'm afraid I couldn't hear very well."

"That's because you weren't paying attention. If you're

"NEVERTHELESS," WILLIAM SAID,
"THE LESSONS WILL CONTINUE."

not going to pay attention, you may as well leave!"

Ashamed, Parthe put her books away and left the room. Though her father was angry, Parthe knew her mother would not be. Sometimes Fanny even found excuses to get Parthe out of lessons.

With Parthe gone, Mr. Nightingale turned to the history lesson. "Open your book to the chapter on Egypt."

This excited Florence. History was her favorite subject. The Egyptian rooms were her favorites when the family went to visit the British Museum.

"Papa, I want to visit the Egyptian rooms again," she said. "And next time, could we see the Elgin Marbles?"

These ancient Greek sculptures came from the Parthenon, a temple on the Acropolis in Athens, Greece. Lord Elgin had obtained permission to display them at the British Museum.

"Someday, Florence, I'll take you to Greece and show you the Parthenon."

After the history lesson was over, Mr. Nightingale told

"PAPA, I WANT TO VISIT THE EGYPTIAN ROOMS AGAIN."

Florence to write an essay in French. He watched her work. She was always eager to learn. She understood things easily and seemed to have an unusual ability in mathematics.

My little May flower is very special indeed, Mr. Nightingale thought to himself.

MY LITTLE MAY FLOWER IS VERY SPECIAL INDEED.

"WHAT A HORRIBLE WASTE OF TIME."

2

God Calls to Florence

As Florence grew older, she was no longer afraid she
was a monster. But she was unhappy with her life, and
sometimes felt she was in the wrong family.

She wanted to do something important with her life,
but her wealth demanded she do nothing more than ride
horses, play piano, and hostess tea parties.

"What a horrible waste of time," she complained, "to
spend my life gossiping over tea!"

The busy social season at Embley bored Florence.
Parthe loved the endless parties and visitors, and fell right
in with her mother and the other ladies.

The older Florence got, the more she fought with her
mother. Mrs. Nightingale blamed her husband for
Florence's behavior.

"You have spoiled her, William," she said, "filling her

head with grand ideas from those silly books of yours."

"Now, Fanny," William soothed. "I know Florence is not the same as Parthe, but I do believe we have a very special daughter. You'll see."

Fanny Nightingale sighed. "Sometimes I feel like I have given birth to a wild swan!"

Florence loved her mother and hated upsetting her. But it saddened Florence to think that her life would consist only of taking care of a husband and children. Not that that was not a worthy occupation, just not something Florence wanted her entire life to focus on.

◆

The Nightingales had tenants on their property at Lea Hurst who were considerably less fortunate than the Nightingales. Florence often went from cottage to cottage taking food and clothing to these poor people. If a baby was born, Florence jumped at the chance to cook and clean for the new mother. And, if someone fell ill, she nursed them back to health.

"Why do you waste your time with the tenants?"

FLORENCE OFTEN WENT FROM COTTAGE TO COTTAGE.

Parthe asked her.

"Helping people makes me feel good and useful."

Florence was often touched and saddened by what she saw in those cottages. She once wrote to a cousin: "I saw a poor woman die before my eyes this summer because there was nothing but fools to sit up with her, who poisoned her as much as if they had given her arsenic."

Fanny firmly objected to Florence's actions. At that time it was customary for rich women to call on the poor, maybe even to take gifts of soup and jam. But Florence's care and concern went far beyond reasonable boundaries as far as Fanny was concerned.

"I'm all for being kind, Florence," she scolded. "But as usual, you are going to extremes. It's just not right for a Nightingale to lower herself to doing housework for the poor."

"Yes, Mama," Florence murmured. But, of course, she continued to help the poor. She didn't know why, she just had to.

"How is it that you know how to cure people and

"I'M ALL FOR BEING KIND, FLORENCE."

animals?" her father once asked.

"I don't really, Papa. I just feed them, make them comfortable, keep them clean, and love them." She shrugged. "Then most of them get better."

When Florence was sixteen, something happened that made her stop doubting herself for good.

She was alone in her room one day when a voice began speaking to her. She didn't tell anyone about it, but in her diary, she wrote: "On February 7, 1837, God spoke to me and called me to His service."

Florence realized once and for all that she was not a monster, just different from Parthe and other girls. And though the voice had not told her exactly what she was to do, God Himself had a mission for her to carry out.

Florence, for the first time in her life, felt content. All she had to do was be patient. God would reveal His plan to her when the time was right. And even though the details were not clear, Florence was delighted to know her life had some meaning and purpose after all. Perhaps she could eventually escape the wealth and self-gratification

"GOD SPOKE TO ME AND CALLED ME TO HIS SERVICE."

so abundant around her.

But she would have to think about that later. God's call had come just as the Nightingale family was planning to tour the continent.

SHE WOULD HAVE TO THINK ABOUT THAT LATER.

"I WILL BE PRESENTED AT COURT ALONG WITH PARTHE."

3
A Grand Young Lady

Fanny Nightingale began to worry that Florence would never find a husband. "She simply must give up these silly ideas of hers. It is time for her to be presented at court."

"I do not want to be presented at court," Florence argued. "It's a ridiculous custom that I do not wish to be part of."

Fanny threw her hands up. She had lived with Florence long enough to know her mind had been made up, though Fanny did bring the topic up from time to time.

When Princess Victoria was crowned Queen of England, Florence changed her mind. The Queen was only a year older, and Florence thought meeting her would be fun.

"Mother," she hesitatingly said, "if it would make you happy, I will be presented at court along with Parthe."

Mrs. Nightingale was delighted! But presenting two

young ladies into society required lots of work. Many parties in the girls' honor would be given. Six more rooms would have to be built onto the house to accommodate all the guests at Embley.

"I want new carpet throughout the house," Fanny told William. "And the ballroom should be remodeled."

Mr. Nightingale put all his skills and time into planning the improvements at Embley. He had time for nothing else, including daily lessons.

"Thank goodness we don't have to sit through those dreadful lectures any more!" Parthe exclaimed.

"I rather miss Papa's lectures," Florence sighed.

The preparations and remodeling would take a year. It would be too uncomfortable to live in the house during the remodeling. Mrs. Nightingale suggested they go to Europe.

"We could take the girls to Paris and introduce them to French society," she told her husband.

"I suppose," Mr. Nightingale said, unenthusiastically.

"But if we went to Italy," she continued, "we could

" SUPPOSE," MR NIGHTINGALE SAID, UNENTHUSIASTICALLY.

show Florence the city where she was born."

At that William Nightingale warmed to the idea. "It has been such a long time since we've seen our friends there."

When the girls heard the news, Parthe squealed with delight.

"Will we be in Rome long enough to visit the Coliseum?" Florence asked.

Fanny and Parthe rolled their eyes.

"Oh, Florence," her mother teased lightly, "your mind is always in your history books."

They spent weeks preparing for the trip. They bought a new carriage and filled their trunks with new dresses and hats. On September 15, 1837, the family set off along with two servants and Mrs. Gale, the girls' nanny.

The Nightingale family delighted in travel; it was their favorite pastime. Florence usually didn't like traveling, but now, secure in the knowledge that God had a significant life planned for her, she could not be miserable no matter how hard she tried.

"...YOUR MIND IS ALWAYS IN YOUR HISTORY BOOKS."

Florence breathed in the beautiful scenery and towns.

The Nightingales planned month-long stays at Nice and Genoa, amidst all the sight-seeing. William Nightingale had sent many letters of introduction to important families in France and Italy. Parthe and Florence Nightingale were to be showered with invitations to picnics and social gatherings.

The hardest part of the trip would be leaving the friends they had made in each city. But the friendliness of those at the next stop would quickly drown out that pain.

Florence spent hours touring the museums of Paris. She even began to enjoy all the dinner parties and balls. The men found Florence charming and attractive. She was soon one of the most popular young ladies in Paris.

Mrs. Nightingale was delighted. "Oh, William, I knew this trip to Europe was an excellent idea. We'll have Florence married in no time."

In Italy, Florence was overwhelmed by the beauty of the city she was named after. She visited all the famous churches, attended balls given by the Grand Duke, and

THE MEN FOUND FLORENCE CHARMING AND ATTRACTIVE.

fell totally in love with the opera.

"Oh, Mother, I have become the biggest music lover in Italy!"

At that time, Italy was under the rule of the Austrian government. Many Italians fighting for independence were imprisoned, others were forced to leave the country.

William Nightingale became friends with many of the Italian freedom fighters.

"Oh, Papa," Florence cried, "they have so much courage. Why must we have everything so easy, when these people have such terrible lives?"

"There will always be poor, wretched people in the world, Florence."

A thought sparked in her mind. Perhaps God's plan was for her to help the poor. She knew that whatever His plan was, it would come to be quite clear when it was time and not a second before He was ready.

The Nightingales traveled to Switzerland in September of 1838, and visited Italian friends who had fled to Geneva. They made new friends and Mr. Nightingale

PERHAPS GOD'S PLAN WAS FOR HER TO HELP THE POOR.

enjoyed himself so much he would have stayed a long time.

But the political situation in Europe was not good. Louis Napoleon Bonaparte was being protected in Switzerland. Like his uncle, Napoleon Bonaparte, Louis wanted to be Emperor of France. He was trying to overthrow the French government, and they wanted the Swiss to release him so they could arrest him.

"I'm afraid there's going to be a war," William Nightingale announced at breakfast one morning. "The people in the city are already afraid French soldiers will invade the city."

Outside, hammers pounded. Wooden barricades were being erected around the entire city.

The Nightingales went back to Paris and watched to see what would happen. Louis Napoleon Bonaparte found safety in England and war was avoided. The social life in Paris returned to normal, and Florence and Parthe again attended numerous parties and balls.

The Nightingale family finally returned to their home in the spring of 1839. Florence had been only seventeen

"I'M AFRAID THERE'S GOING TO BE A WAR."

when the family departed. She had been a shy young lady, and it was amazing to see the sophisticated and self-confident young woman that returned after two years of travel on the continent.

A SELF-CONFIDENT YOUNG WOMAN
RETURNED AFTER TWO YEARS.

"IT IS MY HONOR AND PLEASURE, YOUR MAJESTY."

4
Disharmony

On Queen Victoria's twentieth birthday, Florence and Parthe were presented at court. Florence curtsied in awe to the queen.

"It is my honor and pleasure, Your Majesty," she said politely.

Queen Victoria just smiled. A beautiful ball followed.

In the next week, Florence and Parthe made the rounds of London's social circle. Mrs. Nightingale was pleased and proud. Even Florence was excited by her successful introduction into society.

"But," she said to herself, "I must remind myself of God's call. I must be alert at all times, in case He speaks to me again."

Florence grew worried. It had been two years since God had spoken to her, but she had heard nothing more about what her purpose was to be. Perhaps God had lately found her unworthy, with all her vanity during her coming-out, and all the fancy balls she'd been attending.

Florence was rich, pretty, and popular. She was expected to live a life of ease and luxury. Deciding she'd grown too proud for God to speak to, she vowed to become more humble.

Maybe if I humble myself, she thought, *God will speak to me again.*

◆

In 1840, the Nightingales dined with their neighbor, Lord Palmerston. Another guest was an English Nobleman, Lord Anthony Ashley Cooper. Lord Ashley later became the seventh Earl of Shaftesbury.

Florence was thrilled about meeting him. Lord Ashley devoted his life and wealth to helping the poor. He and Florence had wonderful conversations about their mutual concern for the underprivileged members of society.

FLORENCE WAS THRILLED ABOUT MEETING LORD ASHLEY.

"I am particularly concerned about working conditions in coal mines," Lord Ashley told Florence. "Women and children are working underground in unsafe conditions."

Florence clutched her throat and gasped. "How awful! Can't someone do something?"

Lord Ashley investigated the mines himself and eventually wrote the Mines Act of 1842. The Mines Act would not allow women and children to work underground.

"The government will inspect all mines periodically," Lord Ashley's bill said.

As a result, mine owners were forced to use safety measures, and many serious accidents were avoided. Lord Ashley was not popular with the mine owners, for the loss of child-slave labor and the cost of improvements sharply cut their profits.

Lord Ashley smiled at Florence. "But I'm not out to win popularity contests. I wish only to protect people."

So, Lord Ashley helped the poor people working

"I'M NOT OUT TO WIN POPULARITY CONTESTS."

in factories during the Industrial Revolution. He was also concerned about hospitals and health care in England.

Florence was eager to work with Lord Ashley. She was convinced that she had been called by God to help the sick and the poor. She turned to Lord Ashley for help. He gave her government reports on working conditions and added hospital reports when Florence expressed a desire to become a nurse.

Lord Anthony Ashley Cooper was a strong influence on Florence for many years. Their mutual concern for the welfare of others drew them together.

◆

Florence decided to visit her Aunt Mai in London.

"Oh, Mother," she exclaimed while she was packing. "I just love Aunt Mai's children. Especially little Shore."

Early in her visit to London, Florence was caught up in the enjoyment of festivities to celebrate Queen Victoria's marriage to Prince Albert. But amid all the

"I JUST LOVE AUNT MAI'S CHILDREN."

hoopla, Florence secretly planned to study mathematics.

"Utter nonsense!" Mrs. Nightingale shouted when she heard the news. "A married woman has no need for a knowledge of numbers." Even Florence's father was angry.

But Aunt Mai was more sympathetic. She hired Florence a math tutor. Florence stayed with Aunt Mai for two months, studying math and playing with the children.

Florence returned to Lea Hurst and again took care of the sick villagers. The family was outraged.

"Florence, how could you embarrass us this way? A girl of your status lowering yourself to that level!"

"Mother, you just don't understand my special calling."

"Your calling?" Fanny Nightingale snorted. "What calling?"

"God has spoken to me. He has called me to His service."

Fanny shook her head and stomped from the room.

"MOTHER, YOU JUST DON'T UNDERSTAND MY SPECIAL CALLING."

William Nightingale went to his library and shut the door.

Life in the Nightingale household grew unpleasant. A battle of wills was in progress, and no one was budging. Florence was often ill, nervous, and jumpy during this time. She even had frequent fainting spells.

"All my parents expect of me," Florence told a close friend, "is to get married and have babies. But I know there is a higher purpose for me."

Parties went on at Embley. Florence had attracted a number of men, all anxious to marry her.

Florence's father cornered her one night at a party. "Your mother tells me you're cooking for the poor again."

"But, Papa, they have no one to take care of them when they're sick."

"Your mother is right. A girl of your position has no business among the villagers."

Florence grimaced. "Are you telling me to stop?"

"I'm not telling you to stop caring about people. But

"ARE YOU TELLING ME TO STOP?"

you can give help without getting directly involved. We'll donate more money to the poor villagers. You must remember where you come from, and who you are."

But I do know who I am! Florence wanted to shout. *I am an instrument of God. Will no one ever understand that?*

Florence felt terrible about fighting with her mother and father again. Even Parthe couldn't stay out of it.

"You're hurting Mama and Papa," she criticized. "Can't you just get married, have children, and be happy?"

"No, Parthe, I can't. I have been called to special service."

In 1841 at Christmastime, the Nightingales went to visit the Nicholson family in Surrey, England. Fanny's sister, Anne, had married a Nicholson. Anne's daughter, Marianne, and Florence were great friends.

Eighty people were there that Christmas, enough to put on a performance of *The Merchant of Venice*. Parthe

"YOU'RE HURTING MAMA AND PAPA."

painted scenes and made costumes, while Florence helped the actors memorize their lines.

Besides putting on the play, the youngsters also played games and held a masked ball. In those days, there were no television or video games to entertain the young people!

But the friendship between Marianne and Florence was threatened by a man named Henry Nicholson, Marianne's brother. Henry fell deeply in love with Florence.

"Wouldn't it be simply delightful," Fanny bubbled to her sister Anne, "if Henry and Florence married?"

But Florence did not care for Henry. When he proposed in 1845—one of many men to propose to Florence—she refused him. He drowned five years later, while vacationing in Spain, still in love with Florence Nightingale.

While in Surrey, Florence also grew close to her Aunt Hannah Nicholson. Aunt Hannah took it upon herself to educate Florence in religious matters.

WHEN HENRY PROPOSED IN 1845, SHE REFUSED HIM.

"You must obey your parents, Florence," Aunt Hannah told her.

Florence disagreed. "But, Aunt Hannah, if I do what they wish, I will be unable to follow God's call."

Hannah Nicholson was outraged. "You undutiful child!" Hannah severed the relationship. She refused to see or write to Florence again.

In 1842, Florence met Chevalier Bunsen, the Prussian Ambassador, and his wife in London. The Bunsens grew quite fond of Florence, and she visited them often.

"It is admirable that you seek to help mankind," they told her. "So few people of your stature concern themselves with those less fortunate."

Soon after meeting the Bunsens, Florence was again invited to dinner with Lord Palmerston. There, she met Richard Monckton Milnes.

Richard Monckton Milnes was a young politician who was deeply concerned about many of the issues Florence cared about. Instead of putting youngsters in jails, where

SHE MET RICHARD MONCKTON MILNES.

they would be in the company of criminals, he worked to have them put in reformatories.

"I understand you also have a taste for poetry, Mr Milnes," Florence said.

Richard Monckton Milnes had arranged to have Keats' first book of poems published.

"Quite right," he replied. "And I admire your concern about the poor people, Miss Nightingale. I, too have a soft spot in my heart for them."

As one of the most eligible bachelors in England Richard Milnes was perfect for Florence.

"I'm in love with you, Florence," he finally confessed one evening. "I want to marry you."

"I'm in love with you, too, Richard."

An unspoken "but" hung heavily in the air. Florence did love Richard. But if she married him, her own dreams would never be fulfilled. In those days married women did not work outside the home. If she married Richard, she would be a society wife dedicated to her husband's advancement.

IF SHE MARRIED HIM, HER OWN DREAMS
WOULD NEVER BE FULFILLED.

"I love him too much to say no right away," Florence told a friend. "But I can't say yes, either. This is just too important a matter to give him a definite answer yet."

Summer at Lea Hurst went on. Every day, Florence took food to the poor old women who lived alone. She even rubbed ointment on their aching legs.

When fall came, Florence approached her mother. "I want to stay on here at Lea Hurst for the winter."

"Impossible!" Fanny exclaimed. "You would miss the social season. I will never allow it."

Florence decided that God's mission for her was to relieve the suffering of the poor and the ill. She knew she wanted to work in hospitals.

"But how can I tell that to Mama and Papa?" she asked herself.

◆

In the summer of 1884, American doctor Samuel Gridley Howe visited Florence and her family. He and his wife Julia were touring Europe. Florence grew fond of the doctor and asked him for his help.

"HOW CAN I TELL THAT TO MAMA AND PAPA?"

One morning she hurried downstairs before breakfast. Dr. Howe was waiting in the library, where she had told him to meet her.

"Dr. Howe," she started, "do you think it's wrong of me to want to care for the sick and the poor?"

Dr. Howe thought a moment. "It would be unusual for a woman of your position. But I see nothing wrong about helping others. But I'm afraid I don't understand this desire of yours."

"I feel like God is leading me into this charitable work."

Dr. Howe smiled. "Then, I think you should go ahead!"

Dr. Howe's encouragement helped Florence see that nursing was right for her. But more disappointments were to come.

That summer scarlet fever broke out in the village. Florence was told to stay away from the tenants. She spent all summer inside, feeling useless.

Another year went slowly by. Florence was twenty-five years old. It had been eight years since she had

"THEN I THINK YOU SHOULD GO AHEAD!"

heard God's call.

How much longer before I can fulfill my purpose? she thought anxiously.

HOW MUCH LONGER BEFORE I CAN FULFILL MY PURPOSE?

FLORENCE FELT SHE NEEDED TO KNOW MORE ABOUT NURSIN

5
Breaking the Family Ties

Florence's grandmother fell ill in 1845, giving Florence a chance to prove herself and her skills to her family. The faithful nanny Mrs. Gale grew old, sick, and feeble. Florence cared for the old woman until she died.

"Florence does have a knack for helping those who are ill," Fanny said one evening.

"Yes," William agreed. "From now on when she goes to the village, we will not try to stop her."

Fanny reluctantly agreed. "If you insist, William."

Florence was elated. At last, God had sent her a clear signal of what her purpose was. Caring for her grandmother and Mrs. Gale had made that quite clear to her.

Although in those days formal education was not required for nurses, Florence felt she needed to know more about nursing to be the best she could.

There was a hospital a few miles from Embley, and Florence decided to stay there.

"I am going to study at the Salisbury Infirmary," she announced to her family. "By watching the doctors there, I can be a better nurse."

Her mother chuckled. "Oh, Florence, taking care of sick villagers is one thing, but this. . . .Surely, you can't be serious."

"I am quite serious. I feel God has called me to this service. Watching the doctors as they work at the Salisbury Infirmary will be the best way for me to learn."

"You will disgrace the entire family," her mother grumbled. "What will my friends think if I allow my daughter to go off and do such a thing?"

Parthe, crying, shouted, "You may as well be someone's maid!"

William Nightingale's anger kept him from speaking at all. His daughter was not a common underling suited for this type of work. She was too affluent and too intelligent. The thought of her spending her life scrubbing

"I AM GOING TO STUDY AT THE SALISBURY INFIRMARY."

floors in a filthy public hospital sickened him. Without uttering a word, William turned on his heel and left the room.

Her family's resistance was understandable. The Nightingales were affluent citizens from the upper level of society, and hospitals then were not like they are today. The filthy rooms and wards were cramped spaces overflowing with patients. Rats and mice skittered around the floors, and bugs were often found in the food.

Antiseptics had not yet been discovered and the hospitals were not kept clean so they smelled of death and disease.

The rich cared for their sick at home. The poor went to the hospitals only because they had no choice.

Hospitals were so wretched that few people really wanted to work there. Most nurses were from poor families and were mentally unable to work as maids, household servants, or other more respectable occupations. Many of the nurses drank, or began drinking after working in the hospitals.

HOSPITALS THEN WERE NOT LIKE THEY ARE TODAY.

Nurses were not trained then as they are now. They were often rough and abusive with patients, because no one told them it was wrong. The bedding was seldom changed, and the patients were rarely bathed. Thus, in such filthy conditions, infections spread and more patients died than lived.

Nurses of that time were spat on by society. Being a nurse was a disgrace, not the honorable profession it is now.

"I forbid you to step foot in the Salisbury Infirmary," William bellowed one evening.

"You can keep me out of the Salisbury Infirmary, Father, but you cannot keep me from doing God's work." Florence refused to give up. "If I cannot study hospitals from the inside," she vowed to herself, "then, I shall study them from the outside!"

Unknown to her family, Florence began to collect articles about public health. She received her information from hospitals and government health officials. After a short time, she owned more than one thousand

"I FORBID YOU TO STEP FOOT IN THE SALISBURY INFIRMARY."

health-related documents. After her family went to bed each night, Florence read until her eyes burned and ached.

◆

Richard Monckton Milnes had been waiting seven years for Florence to answer his marriage proposal. He was growing impatient.

"I have waited a long time, my dear Flo," he said softly. "You most certainly know how much I love you."

"And I love you, Richard." Florence meant it. She loved Richard more than anyone, but she did not feel God was leading her toward marriage and motherhood.

"I will not wait any longer." Richard said. "Yes or no, I demand an answer."

Much as she loved him, she knew she would be a miserable wife. If she could not pursue the work God planned for her, her life would lose all meaning.

"I'm sorry, Richard," she said, her lower lip trembling. "I can't marry anyone, not even you who I love so very much."

Richard was crushed, hopeless. "But if you love me

"I WILL NOT WAIT ANY LONGER."

so much, why will you not marry me?"

Florence told him of God's call. She told him of her desire to be a nurse to help the sick and the poor.

Though still brokenhearted, Richard nodded and hugged her. "Even I cannot compete with God, dear Florence. If this is what you want, then I wish you all the success and happiness that you do so deserve."

Richard Monckton Milnes hugged Florence Nightingale once more, then turned and walked out of her life.

"Florence!" Fanny yelled up the stairs. "Come down here this instant!"

Florence dreaded every step downward. "Yes, Mama?" she squeaked.

"Is it true that you refused Richard Milnes' marriage proposal?"

Florence took a breath and bravely jutted her chin out. "Yes, Mother, it is true."

Fanny clenched her hands and her face reddened. "You have to be the most selfish young woman in England! A

"...YOU REFUSED RICHARD MILNES' MARRIAGE PROPOSAL?"

fine young man like Richard, and you refuse him!"

"But, Mother, what I really want is—"

Fanny silenced Florence with an upturned hand. "Enough! I have listened to all the nursing nonsense I can bear. I will hear no more of it."

Fanny stomped from the room, leaving her daughter standing at the bottom of the steps.

The strain between Florence and her family was so great that Florence's health faltered. She was near collapse. If not for loving, understanding friends, she would have fallen to despair.

"We've planned a tour of Egypt and Greece, Flo," they said to her. "Join us. It will be good for you."

In Athens, Greece, Florence was awestruck by the Parthenon.

"Oh!" she sighed. "It is even more magnificent than I dreamed. Seeing it for real after all my years of studying it in books almost moves me to tears."

After that trip with her friends, Florence continued to travel.

"IT IS EVEN MORE MAGNIFICENT THAN I DREAMED."

The small village of Kaiserwerth along the Rhine River in Germany, was a catalyst for Florence Nightingale. She visited a hospital there. Its founder, a Lutheran minister named Theodore Fliedner, offered to show her the hospital. He opened one door and Florence peered in.

"This, Miss Nightingale, is where our orphan children sleep."

Florence gasped softly. These children looked and acted nothing like English orphans. These children appeared happy and serene in their little beds.

"We almost always have more patients than we can handle," Pastor Fliedner explained. "A few years ago, I began training nurses at a school housed in the Lutheran Church. I hope to add to my staff here."

Florence's ears perked up. "Oh, please, Pastor Fliedner, could I train there, too?"

Pastor Fliedner's eyebrows shot up. "But most of our girls come from the farms around the village. Are you sure a girl of your stature wants to spend her days from sunrise to sunset scrubbing floors?"

"H, PLEASE, PASTOR FLIEDNER, COULD I TRAIN THERE TOO?"

"It is the work I have been chosen to do," Florence replied.

◆

"I am returning to Germany," Florence told her family when she was back home. "I am going to train at a nursing school founded by a Lutheran minister. It's in Kaiserwerth."

"I will not discuss this with you again," Fanny said.

"But Kaiserwerth is different from our English hospitals. It is clean and cheerful, and the nurses are respectable churchwomen."

But Florence's family ignored her arguments. Florence resumed the living pace at Embley.

William and Fanny Nightingale felt Florence should be punished for sneaking off to work at Kaiserwerth in the first place.

"As punishment for your so-called holiday in Germany," William said, "you will devote the next six months entirely to your sister, Parthe."

As the weeks passed, Florence felt trapped and resentful. Florence was determined to work at Kaiserwerth

FLORENCE'S FAMILY IGNORED HER ARGUMENTS.

again when Fanny, as already planned, would take the girls to Germany in 1851.

Parthe, too, was upset. The sisters had been close, and Parthe tried to talk Florence out of returning to work at Kaiserwerth.

"But, Flo, just see how much this silly idea has hurt and angered Mama and Papa."

"Parthe, I'm not doing it to hurt them. And it's not a silly idea. I have been called to this work."

Though she wanted her family's approval, Florence knew they would continue to hinder her steps toward nursing. She had no choice. She would have to break away from them and follow her own heart and God's plan for her.

◆

While visiting London, Florence met Dr. Elizabeth Blackwell. Elizabeth Blackwell had been the first woman in the United States to become a doctor.

"My family also objected," she told Florence. "They tried to keep me from going to medical school."

FLORENCE MET DR. ELIZABETH BLACKWELL.

Florence nodded in sympathy. Dr. Blackwell studied her a moment.

"You have to follow your own heart, my dear Florence. If you feel called and ignore the call, your life will be nothing but torment. No matter if your parents are pleased or not."

Dr. Elizabeth Blackwell became Florence's role model. She had given Florence the courage to seek her own dream. But Florence felt simply terrible that she and Parthe continued to fight. She wanted Parthe's blessing, but they were too different to understand each other. Parthe was quite satisfied at home and thought Florence should be, too.

"Mama and Papa give us everything we want and need, and you still slouch around here like a sick and sad little puppy. What does it take to make you happy?"

"We have everything we need, Parthe, but all around us people are suffering. They're poor, sick, and lonely."

"There will always be poor, unfortunate souls in the world, Florence. And you can't save them all."

"U HAVE TO FOLLOW YOUR OWN HEART, MY DEAR FLORENCE."

"But I can save some of them," Florence replied stubbornly.

Florence believed in her heart that if she could ease one person's suffering, God's plan for her would be fulfilled. She would have no contentment until then.

"When I finish my training," she told Parthe, "I'll live in London and work in a hospital."

"Mama and Papa will never allow it."

Florence gazed sadly at her sister. "I'm afraid I'm not asking for their permission."

But the Nightingales managed to keep her at home for another couple of years. During her two-year "captivity," Florence even considered becoming a nun. She went to speak to the cardinal about it.

Cardinal Manning smiled at Florence. "Florence, dear, I know your heart is pure, but I don't believe this would be a true conversion. But, if you like, I can arrange for you to work with the Sisters of Charity in Paris."

Florence was elated. "Oh! Thank you so much, Cardinal Manning!"

"I'M AFRAID I'M NOT ASKING FOR THEIR PERMISSION."

But before she could leave for Paris, William Nightin gale fell ill, and Florence had to stay home to nurse him. She was preparing to leave again in 1852 when Parthe had a nervous breakdown. Again, Florence was expected to stay home until her sister was well.

Sir James Clark, the Queen's official physician, took care of Parthe. "She cannot live a normal life in the shadow of Florence," he told Fanny and William Nightingale.

Florence finally felt free to go, but Fanny still tried desperately to cling to her younger daughter.

"I'll give you the country house my aunt left me," Fanny pleaded. "You can establish your own hospital and train the nurses yourself. I'll pay for everything."

"No, Mama. I have to be on my own. I have to go where I feel God is leading me."

Florence went to Paris, where she stayed with a friend for a month before entering the convent of the Sisters of Charity.

"Florence is in Paris buying new dresses," Fanny fibbed to her society friends. "She'll be home soon."

"I HAVE TO GO WHERE I FEEL GOD IS LEADING ME."

But Florence returned home only briefly, to nurse her Grandmother Shore when she fell ill. After Grandmother Shore died, Florence was offered the position of superintendent of the Institution for the Care of Sick Gentlewomen in Distressed Circumstances.

"The job is a public service," she was told. "You will not be paid, and you will be responsible for your own expenses, as well as those of your matron chaperone."

Florence, of course, cared more about health reform than money. She accepted the job and on August 12, 1853, moved into the Institution's headquarters at Harley Street.

Florence's months at Harley Street were both exhilarating and exhausting. She worked from dawn to nightfall, but her heart was full of joy.

In a letter to her mother, she wrote: *I am deeply interested in everything here and am well in mind and body. I now know what it is to love life. I wish for no other world but this.*

The Nightingales read Florence's letter with great disappointment. They had hoped the long hours and hard

I WISH FOR NO OTHER WORLD BUT THIS.

work would change Florence's mind. But she seemed more determined than ever to be a nurse.

William Nightingale finally accepted defeat. After all, Florence was his daughter and he adored her. It had become clear that she would lead her own life, despite their objections. He decided to pay her an income.

"Spend it any way you wish," he wrote to her.

Florence was ecstatic. Financially independent, she would be free to lead her own life. At last!

It had been sixteen years since Florence had heard God's call. Now, she felt, was the time to begin her mission.

NOW, SHE FELT, WAS THE TIME TO BEGIN HER MISSION.

"I AM SO PROUD OF YOU, FLORENCE."

6
Heading to the Crimea

Florence's job at the institution was an important one. Following that job, she was put in charge of a nursing home in London. The job carried a great deal of responsibility. Florence was nervous, but felt confident that God would stand by her as she performed His work.

"I am so proud of you, Florence," Aunt Mai told her. "And happy that you have sought your own desires."

Aunt Mai had supported Florence throughout her struggle with her family. But Mai was not the only one who believed in Florence and her mission for the Lord.

Florence's closest friends also worked to improve the way hospitals cared for the sick. Sidney Herbert, Britain's Secretary of War, ran the army hospitals.

"I admire Miss Nightingale's determination," he told a colleague. "I respect her knowledge of how hospitals work.

For someone who taught herself, she is quite brilliant."

♦

On November 30, 1853, Czar Nicholas I of Russia ordered one of his ships to attack a Turkish fleet in the Crimea. The Turkish fleet was sunk and, a continent away, Florence Nightingale's life was forever changed by the event.

Czar Nicholas I planned to make his Russian Navy as strong as those in Britain and France. Nicholas set up a naval base in the Russian city of Sebastapol, located on the tip of the Crimea and extending into the Black Sea. The only path through the Black Sea to the Mediterranean Sea was a narrow strip of water governed by Turkey. When his ships were bottle-necked there, Czar Nicholas I was irate. "Then I shall have to conquer Turkey!" he raged at his naval officers.

The Turkish government sought help from their allies. On March 27, 1854, Turkey, Britain, and France declared war on Russia.

The Allies were victorious on the ground in the early

TURKEY, BRITAIN AND FRANCE DECLARED WAR ON RUSSIA.

battles, and the British rejoiced at the news. But many men had died on the battlefield, and others had died from cholera and other horrible diseases.

William H. Russell, a reporter for the *London Times*, was one of the first to ever report events in a war. The reports he sent from the Crimea were embarrassing to the British government.

"The British Army is poorly organized," he wrote. "The wounded get sloppy and sometimes inhumane care, and medical supplies are scarce. Suffering is great. . . And hundreds of men could have been saved with better organization and more sanitary medical care."

People were outraged after hearing Russell's reports. "Something has to be done!" was a comment often heard on the streets of Britain. "The government owes us an explanation for all this!"

Florence's friend Sidney Herbert shouldered much of the criticism.

The *Times* started a collection for the purchase of medical supplies. Donations came from all over the country,

"THE BRITISH ARMY IS POORLY ORGANIZED," HE WROTE.

many from people who had sons, husbands, or brothers fighting in the Crimea.

Sidney Herbert's plan was to send a committee to the British Army hospital in the Turkish village of Scutari.

"The person who leads this group," he told Florence, "has to be able to get the facts straight and tell me how bad it really is. It is most important that the person know about how hospitals are run. The hospital at Scutari will need to be reorganized."

"I agree, Sidney," Florence said. "I will do my best to help you find someone suitable."

Sidney had already thought of someone—Florence Nightingale. But he hesitated to ask her, because there was a problem. Nurses had never been permitted to work in army hospitals.

Still, Sidney Herbert reasoned, *this is a desperate situation. We need skilled people to care for these men. That is all that matters.*

In October, 1854, Sidney Herbert wrote to Florence Nightingale: "There is but one person in England that I

HE HAD ALREADY THOUGHT OF SOMEONE—
FLORENCE NIGHTINGALE.

know of who would be capable of organizing and superintending such a scheme. That person is you, Florence."

Florence stared at the letter in disbelief. Sidney Herbert was asking her to do this important work. Praise God, her purpose had come!

"You will face a horrible task," Herbert warned her in his letter. "You will need great courage and endless energy. But this is your chance to prove what women are capable of."

◆

"I cannot believe our Florence has been chosen for this," Fanny said when the Nightingales had heard the news.

"Indeed," William said proudly. "I always told you Florence was special. It is a great honor."

"The whole country is buzzing about it," Parthe added.

"They are saying Florence is the first woman in history chosen to represent the British government. Is that true, Papa?"

"Yes, Parthe, it is."

The Nightingales beamed. It appeared they now had a

PRAISE GOD, HER PURPOSE HAD COME!

◆

...t over Florence's chosen occupation.

◆

Florence was not impressed by her appointment. She felt God had given her a job to do, and she intended to do it well. And she had so much to do before leaving, there was no time for thoughts of grandeur. It would not be easy to find nurses willing to accompany her on such a dangerous mission, so far from home.

"This is an important step for women," she said to prospective nurses. "If we succeed, nurses will never again be scorned or ill-treated. We have an opportunity to make a leap forward."

◆

On October 21, 1854, Florence Nightingale and thirty-eight nurses sailed to Constantinople. With her, Florence carried a small black pocketbook that contained three letters; one from her mother, one from Richard Monckton Milnes, and one from Cardinal Manning.

Monday morning, Fanny wrote to her daughter. *God speed you on your errand of mercy, my own dearest child.*

"THIS IS AN IMPORTANT STEP FOR WOMEN."

I know He will, for He has given you such loving friends, and they will always be at your side to help in all your difficulties.

Richard Monckton Milnes' letter spoke of his continued love for Florence, and of his disappointment over her refusing his marriage proposal. *I hear you are going East,* he wrote. *You can undertake that, when you could not undertake me. God bless you, dear friend, wherever you go.*

Cardinal Manning had faith in God to watch over Florence and her nurses. *God will keep you, and my prayer for you will be that your one object of Worship, Pattern of Imitation, and Source of Consolation, and strength may be the Sacred Heart of Our Divine Lord.*

◆

Before Florence had left for Constantinople, English novelist Elizabeth Gaskell had described her as "tall; very slight and willowy; thick shortish rich, brown hair; very delicate coloring; grey eyes which are pensive, and tend to droop, but which when they choose can be the

GOD WILL KEEP YOU

merriest eyes I ever saw."

Mrs. Gaskell had visited the Nightingales at Lea Hurst while Florence had been taking a short vacation from Harley Street. But Mrs. Gaskell had seen other things in Florence as well.

"She stands perfectly alone," Elizabeth Gaskell went on, "halfway between God and His creatures. She used to go a great deal among the villagers. . . . One woman lost a boy seven years ago of white swelling in the knee. Florence Nightingale went twice a day to dress it. The mother speaks of Florence Nightingale as a heavenly angel. She will not go among the villagers now because her heart and soul are (consumed) by her hospital plans. She is so excessively gentle in voice, manner, and movement, that one never feels the unbendableness when one is near her. Her powers are astonishing."

Florence Nightingale was indeed a strong, single-minded woman. She knew her purpose, and ignored anything not relevant to that purpose. The British Army Medical Department would soon find out how strong and

"HER POWERS ARE ASTONISHING."

single-minded Florence Nightingale was.

◆

Florence could see Scutari from the deck of the ship. The hospital had once been an Army barracks for the Turkish soldiers.

None of the news reports had prepared Florence for the filth that greeted her at Scutari. An open sewer that had never been drained flowed beneath the hospital. A horrible stench wafted upward, throughout the building.

Nearly four miles of patients occupied the hospital. Only a few had beds, the others lay on straw mattresses on the bare floor. Rats and insects scuttled about, increasing the soldiers' misery.

"Oh!" Florence gasped. "Some of them don't even have blankets to cover themselves!"

Many of the patients, some of them quite obviously still awaiting treatment, shivered half-naked in corners.

Florence was appalled by the kitchen, too. There was not enough food and no eating utensils. The soldiers received a small piece of boiled meat each day, which they

ORENCE COULD SEE SCUTARI FROM THE DECK OF THE SHIP.

had to tear apart with their fingers or teeth. The soldiers who were too sick to feed themselves were give the thin broth left in the pot after the meat was boiled.

Florence was given her own "room"—a tiny cubicle containing an army cot, a writing table, a lamp, and a crude dresser. Her nurses were given quarters in five cramped rooms.

Many of the army doctors disliked Florence, and resented the presence of the other nurses.

"She will hinder our work," growled one.

"I don't see how a bunch of women are going to make things any better," grumbled another.

Some of the doctors tried to prevent Florence and her nurses from doing their jobs. But then a series of events proved to the doctors how much they needed the nurses' help.

At the Battle of Balaklava, a brigade of British soldiers on horseback got their orders confused and plowed right into the Russian troops. Many were butchered.

Florence and her nurses saved as many as they could;

FLORENCE AND HER NURSES SAVED AS MANY AS THEY COULD.

probably more than would have been saved by the doctors alone.

I cannot believe the brutality, Florence wrote home. *We are all God's children, yet we hack at one another as if we are cattle to be slaughtered.*

Soon after the tragedy at Balaklava, an epidemic of cholera broke out. Thousands of soldiers fell ill.

◆

Howling winds announced the arrival of winter to the Crimea. The British soldiers crowded into the city of Sebastopol frozen in the bitter cold.

"Where is our shipment of food and clothing?" one officer demanded.

"It sank during the hurricane last week," a colleague sadly informed him.

Florence wrote to a doctor friend at Harley Street about conditions at Scutari. *We have had such a sea in the Bosphorous,* she stated referring to the hurricane, *and the Turks. . .for whom we are fighting, carry in our wounded so cruelly, that they arrive in a state of agony.*

HOWLING WINDS ANNOUNCED THE ARRIVAL OF WINTER.

One amputated stump died two hours after he arrived, one compound fracture (died) just as we were getting him into bed—in all, twenty-four cases have died on the day of landing. The dysentery cases have died at the rate of one in two. We have four miles of beds eighteen inches apart. The wounded are lining up to our very door, and we are landing five hundred and forty more from the "Andes." Every ten minutes an orderly runs to fetch another patient, and we have to go cram lint into a wound till a surgeon can be sent for and stop the bleeding as well as we can.

But the stubbornness of the doctors prevented Florence and her companions from doing their jobs properly. Rather than being permitted to nurse the patients, they'd been reduced to mere housekeepers.

Unfortunately, conditions at Scutari did not improve soon. Wounded men continued to pour in. Medicine was scarce near the battle sites, and even healthy men became ill.

Defeated, the head officer said, "These men will have

THEY'D BEEN REDUCED TO MERE HOUSEKEEPERS.

to be shipped across the Black Sea, and placed in the hospital at Sebastapol."

"We have more soldiers in this hospital than on the battlefields," one doctor at Scutari fretted.

"It is physically impossible for us to care for all of them alone," moaned another.

"What are you suggesting?" barked the first doctor.

The younger doctor shuffled his feet. "I think we need to admit to Miss Nightingale that we need the help of her nurses after all.

The older doctor nodded numbly. "You tell her."

◆

Given permission finally to pursue her work, Florence scurried around the hospital like a mad woman. She put the women to work on improving living conditions at the hospital.

"I want you to take cloth," she told some of them, "and stuff them with straw. They won't be like home, but will make better beds and mattresses than the floor."

Florence told the kitchen help to cook thick, nourishing

"... THAT WE NEED THE HELP OF HER NURSES AFTER ALL."

soups, in addition to the boiled meat. "And make hearty puddings for those too weak to eat anything more substantial.

"And before having their wounds attended to," she told her nurses, "each patient must be washed."

"But, Miss Nightingale, many of the men feel too disgusting to let us near them."

"Then we must assure them we have strong stomachs. Just think of all the horrible things we have seen here already! A little dirt is nothing compared to that."

Florence knew it would be difficult for the nurses to win the respect of the doctors. "You must remember we are here to help the doctors, not to interfere. You must follow any order a doctor gives you."

Despite the feelings of the doctors, the patients grew quite fond of Florence Nightingale. Every evening she carried a lamp and walked throughout the wards, checking on the men before she went to bed.

More than two thousand men died at Scutari, though the number most likely would have been higher without

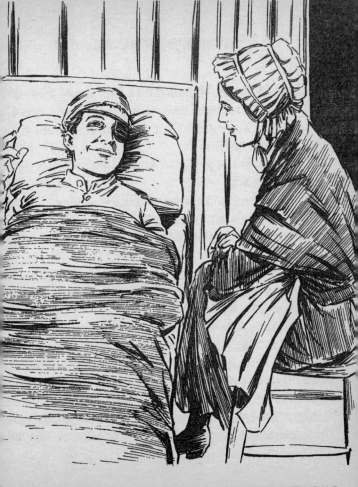

E PATIENTS GREW QUITE FOND OF FLORENCE NIGHTINGALE.

the help of Florence Nightingale and her nurses. Florence often sat at the soldiers' bedsides and held their hands till the end. She wrote down their final words and sent them along to their families.

"She was a saint to us," said one soldier who survived the Crimean War.

Many of the soldiers were amazed at how cheerful Florence remained amidst the horror.

"She would laugh and joke with us when we were down."

"She was a blessed angel sent from heaven."

The men respected Florence so much, they would never swear or drink while she was around.

A valuable Aide at Scutari, named Macdonald, described Florence: "She is a 'Ministering Angel' without any exaggeration in these hospitals, and as her slender form glides quietly along each corridor every poor fellow's face softens with gratitude at the sight of her. When all the medical officers have retired for the night and silence and darkness have settled down upon those miles of prostrate sick, she

"SHE IS A 'MINISTERING ANGEL'."

may be observed alone with a little lamp in her hand, making her solitary rounds."

It was through those "solitary rounds" Macdonald wrote of that Florence Nightingale became known as the "Lady with the Lamp."

"LADY WITH THE LAMP."

CONDITIONS AT THE HOSPITAL DID SLOWLY IMPROVE.

7

A Light in the Dark

Florence worked nearly twenty-four hours a day to care for the soldiers. The devotion and tenderness she had always showered on those she cared about was now directed at the wounded soldiers.

Florence's stubbornness had driven her family nearly to despair most of her life. But conditions at Scutari were so dreadful, her stubbornness became a great tool. Someone of weaker character would not have stayed there long.

All her troubles with her family had made Florence a strong and willful person. She was often outspoken, but was also a natural-born leader. Her grasp of mathematics helped her to keep everything running smoothly.

Conditions at the hospital did slowly improve. "The soldiers already have everything they need," Florence had been told, before leaving England. Still, Florence had used her own money to buy additional supplies. And a good thing she had!

She quickly learned the truth in the Crimea. The soldiers had no bedding or eating utensils, and many of them wore the same filthy, tattered clothes every day.

"This is a disgrace," she said, "to let God's creatures live such a life."

Florence handed out the supplies she had brought. When they were gone she ordered more, again using her own money. It wasn't long before the hospital depended on her for supplies.

A reporter from the *London Times* came to visit the hospital, bringing money the *Times* had collected to buy medical supplies.

"Government officials are telling us the hospitals have everything they need," he informed Florence. "They suggested we use the money to build a church instead."

Florence was angry, though not surprised. "God's work can be done in a hospital just as much as in a church. And I have begged the government officials to come and see

FLORENCE WAS ANGRY, THOUGH NOT SURPRISED.

conditions for themselves. We are constantly running out of supplies."

The numerous rules and regulations about sending supplies to the army frustrated Florence. She had to fill out dozens of forms. While Florence was tangled up in the red tape, shiploads of food often spoiled while sitting in the harbor.

"Meanwhile, these men are starving to death," she raged.

Florence and her nurses took the money from the *Times* and went to the markets at Constantinople. They bought fifty thousand shirts for the men. Over time, they bought sheets, socks, towels, eating utensils, blankets, and other items.

In December, the head doctor called Florence aside. "Five hundred new patients will arrive in about a month."

Florence was aghast. "But we have no room for another five hundred men!" They are already packed together like matchsticks!

The doctor shrugged. "I'm afraid my hands are tied,

"I'M AFRAID MY HANDS ARE TIED."

Miss Nightingale."

One wing of the hospital had been destroyed by fire. Florence got an idea! "If we could rebuild that wing," she told one official, "we would have room for almost a thousand more men."

"With all the red tape and work, Miss Nightingale, that would take a year."

"But the additional men will be here in one month!"

"I'm sorry, Miss Nightingale, it's just not possible."

Florence knelt at her bedside that night. "Please, Lord," she prayed. "You have sent me to help these men, but it all seems so impossible. Tell me how to help them."

The next morning, Florence was more determined than ever to have that wing rebuilt in time to receive the new patients. She now felt nothing was impossible. She managed to persuade the British ambassador to give her money, then she hired Turkish builders.

But things did not go as she had planned.

"Miss Nightingale," one of her nurses said breathlessly, one afternoon. "Come and see."

FLORENCE KNELT AT HER BEDSIDE THAT NIGHT.

"What is it?" Florence asked, following the flustered young lady.

"The workmen have gone on strike! The wing will never be finished in time. What will we do?"

"God will provide a way for us to do our work."

Shortly after the workers went on strike, the British ambassador withdrew his offer to finance the project.

Undaunted, Florence hired two hundred other workers and paid them with her own money. Work on the burned wing was finished just in time for the arrival of the new patients!

◆

Florence was a high energy person. But after months of working sixteen to twenty-hour days, she grew exhausted.

"You should rest more, Miss Nightingale," her nurses urged her. "We can each add a couple of hours to our shifts."

Florence smiled and shook her head. "I couldn't ask you to do that for me. But don't worry, I'll be fine."

But Florence wasn't fine. She soon grew ill. Aunt Mai

FLORENCE GREW EXHAUSTED.

left her family in England and went to the Crimea to take care of her niece.

"Florence," Aunt Mai scolded, "you cannot do God's work if you are ill. You must rest more."

"But I must continue working, Aunt Mai, my nurses and the soldiers need me."

"You will continue working, Florence, but fewer hours please. I will stay until I'm positive you are well enough."

"But you have a family."

"And you are part of my family, darling Florence," Aunt Mai insisted.

The two shared Florence's closet-sized room, squeezing an extra bed between Florence's bed and writing table.

"The doctors gave us tiny quarters," she explained to Aunt Mai, "probably in the hopes we'd get fed up and leave.

"But we have managed to make our rooms rather cozy."

◆

Florence nursed patients all day long. Then she would

"FLORENCE, YOU CANNOT DO GOD'S WORK IF YOU ARE ILL."

sit at her writing table and by candlelight, write letters.

She wrote letters to the families of soldiers who had died, sometimes including their last words or messages they wanted sent to loved ones. She wrote to Sidney Herbert, telling him about her work, and suggesting ways to improve conditions at the hospital.

Aside from supply shortages, she wrote, *our main problem is cleanliness. I don't see how these men can get better while living in filthy surroundings.*

Florence frequently worked through the night. At dawn she would lie down and try to sleep for a few hours before starting all over again.

"Flo," Aunt Mai said one night, "let me finish that letter. You've hardly slept at all this week."

"Thank you, Aunt Mai, but I have to write this one myself."

Florence had much to tell Sidney Herbert in her monthly letter to him.

Queen Victoria has even shown interest in this hospital, she wrote him. *And the men who are recovered have*

QUEEN VICTORIA HAS EVEN SHOWN
INTEREST IN THIS HOSPITAL.

a place to stay, where they can relax a little before returning to battle. There, they have books to read, and the men often gather for tea and conversation.

Prior to this, the only places men could meet were bars. They would drink up most of their army pay, and their families in England saw little of it.

Even when they do send their money home, Florence continued to Sidney, *their families sometimes never receive it.* Sometimes the money was stolen through postal workers and other unscrupulous people.

Florence started collecting their pay and sent it to England herself. She finally persuaded Queen Victoria to create special postal services for the soldiers.

Queen Victoria greatly admired Florence Nightingale, and the work she had done. She wrote to Florence in December, 1855.

You have done wonderful work, Miss Nightingale. It is my wish to send the soldiers a gift of some kind. I would greatly welcome your suggestions.

Florence had long been disturbed by the way the

QUEEN VICTORIA GREATLY ADMIRED FLORENCE NIGHTINGALE.

soldiers were paid. If soldiers were ill and unable to fight, they were paid less than the soldiers who had been wounded in battle.

I feel this is extremely unfair, Florence wrote to Queen Victoria. *After all, aren't the ill soldiers fighting alongside the others? I think your greatest gift would be to pay them all the same amount.*

Queen Victoria agreed. She had the system changed so that each soldier was paid equally.

◆

As the months passed, the patients were eating healthy food, given clean clothes and sheets, and each had a bed. The hospital, as well, was scrubbed clean each day.

In the 1850s, painkilling drugs were not available. Doctors performed surgery without anesthetics, on the patient's own bed, and in full view and earshot of the other patients

"It frightens the other men to see and hear," she told one doctor. "I will use my own money to buy screens to put up around the beds when an operation is being performed."

"I WILL USE MY OWN MONEY TO BUY SCREENS."

Florence later brought in special tables for use during operations. She then turned her attention to the sewer under the hospital.

"I want it drained and disinfected," she ordered.

After this was done, the death rate dropped eighty percent.

◆

"What are you thinking about, Miss Nightingale?" a nurse asked one afternoon.

Florence stood in the center of one of the wards, thoughtfully gazing at the soldiers in their beds.

"We have men with highly contagious diseases lying right beside those with battle wounds."

"Yes?" the young nurse prompted.

Florence shook her head. "There's just something not quite right about that."

Florence decided to put the wounded men in one ward and those with infectious diseases in another. Doing this, the number of deaths at Scutari dropped even lower.

Florence Nightingale was responsible for incredible

"I WANT IT DRAINED AND DISINFECTED."

changes at Scutari. She had become a symbol of hope for the soldiers. Their spirits rose, and they began to believe they would live through the horrible war after all.

The soldiers named her the "Angel of the Crimea." In the evening hours, they would eagerly await the glow of her lamp as she checked on them for the final time of that day. Some men even kissed her shadow as she passed by their beds.

"There is our Lady with the Lamp," one man said as Florence stepped into the ward one evening.

In the afternoons, laughter could be heard and occasionally, singing burst from one of the groups the men had formed. The men played chess and dominoes. Some of the healthier ones played outdoor games on pleasant days.

◆

Florence Nightingale became a great heroine in England. Songs were written about her. Baby girls were named for her. Racehorses and ships were even given her name.

The public wanted to know everything there was to

SHE HAD BECOME A SYMBOL OF HOPE FOR THE SOLDIERS.

know about her. Leaflets of her life story sold on the streets for a penny. Newspapers published any minor detail about her work in the Crimea as well as a number of stories about the sacrifices she had made in her life.

People bought colored pictures of Florence to hang on their walls. Peddlers in London sold Florence Nightingale statues.

The Nightingales were delighted, having given up their fight against her. Many letters were sent to Embley.

Parthe personally answered every piece of fan mail Florence received.

Florence herself remained untouched by fame.

"I have no time for personal glory," she insisted. "Men are still dying in the Crimea. I have much more of God's work to do."

"I HAVE NO TIME FOR PERSONAL GLORY."

FLORENCE TRAVELLED TO HOSPITALS THROUGHOUT THE CRIM

8
Homecoming

By the spring of 1855, things at Scutari had greatly improved.

"I wish to visit other hospitals," Florence told the head doctor. "Hospitals closer to the battlefields."

On May 5, 1855, Florence crossed the Black Sea to Sebastapol, on the war front. On shore, soldiers cheered and threw bouquets of flowers to her.

Doctors at these hospitals reacted the same as the doctors at Scutari had at first. They were angry and resentful of Florence's presence.

"We don't need that meddling woman here!" they grumbled. "She'll do nothing but cause trouble and complicate our procedures here."

Florence ignored them and travelled to hospitals throughout the Crimea on horseback. She was often pelted with freezing rainstorms.

Chilled to the bone and worn out, Florence collapsed, gravely ill with Crimean fever and was expected to die.

"Don't let our Lady die!" soldiers at Scutari wept.

People on the streets of London hugged each other in shocked grief. Their national heroine would soon be passing into the hands of the Lord she had worked so hard for.

But in a couple of weeks, Florence slowly got better.

Queen Victoria received a cable and announced the good news to the English people. The people in the streets of London hugged again, this time with great joy and thankfulness in their hearts.

Admirers throughout the country sent money in to support Florence's continued work. Later the money, known as the Nightingale Fund, was used to start the first training school for nurses.

"I cannot die yet," Florence told friends. "I don't feel that I have yet completed the work God has prepared me

FLORENCE COLLAPSED, AND WAS EXPECTED TO DIE.

for." She soon returned to Scutari.

By fall, the war was almost over. The British had conquered the Russians at Sebastapol. Fewer and fewer patients arrived at Scutari.

A peace treaty was signed on March 30, 1856. The sick and injured soldiers were sent home. The last patient left the hospital on July 16.

Florence knelt for the last time in her tiny little room at Scutari.

"Thank You, Lord, for bringing this horrible war to a close. But, somehow, I still feel my work is incomplete. I know there is more you have planned for me to do. I pray for you to show me the way."

Florence helped her nurses get ready to return home, then she herself prepared to go. She stood in the empty ward, thinking of the men who had died, and those who had returned home to their families.

"God bless and be with every one of them," Florence said, her voice echoing in the hollow room.

◆

"THANK YOU, LORD, FOR BRINGING
THIS HORRIBLE WAR TO A CLOSE."

Several weeks later, William, Fanny, and Parthe Nightingale sat in their parlor at Lea Hurst.

"I can't wait until Florence gets home," Parthe said. "I have missed our chats." She grinned. "I have even missed our arguments."

William Nightingale chuckled. "Your sister is coming home a national heroine."

"And overworked and overtired," Fanny added in a motherly tone.

A moment later, they were jolted by a shriek. They rushed to find their housekeeper staring outside the window.

"It's our little Miss Florence," she exclaimed. "She's come home at last!"

After hugs, kisses, and questions, William admonished Florence. "How did you sneak home? A special welcome has been planned for you. Army bands in London are waiting to greet you."

Florence snorted. "I have no desire for parades and speeches. When I left Constantinople, I used the name

"HOW DID YOU SNEAK HOME?"

Miss Smith. No one recognized me, so I was able to slip quietly into England. I caught a train from the ship, then walked here."

"My sneaky little maiden!" William said, grinning.

It had been more than two years since the Nightingales had seen Florence. Fanny was alarmed by how thin, tired, and ill her youngest daughter looked.

"You have worked hard during this war," Fanny said. "You have earned an extended vacation. You must rest and let your health return."

"But, Mama," Florence argued, "I can't rest now."

"But, Florence, you simply must!"

"The people of England trust me now. Now they will listen to my views on hospital conditions and medical practices. The time for me to suggest changes is now, while that awful war is still fresh in everyone's mind."

Florence had begun to think of the men at Scutari as family. Thousands of her "family" members had died in the Crimea.

"Many of them died from diseases and improper medi-

"BUT MAMA," FLORENCE ARGUED, "I CAN'T REST NOW."

cal care," she explained to her mother, "and not from their wounds. Diseases that could have been controlled, and medical care that could have been better."

Fanny Nightingale patted her daughter's hand. "I know, dear, it must have been awful for you. But try to forget that now."

Florence stood and spun around to look at her mother. "No, Mama, I shall never forget it! And if I can do anything about it, it won't happen again!"

Even though the Nightingales were proud of Florence, they were still somewhat bitter that she had rebelled against them. And Parthe still held an inkling of jealousy toward her sister.

It wasn't until in 1857, when Parthe was about to marry, that a genuine reconciliation was reached.

Parthe was to marry Sir Henry Verney, a fifty-six-year-old widower who had once proposed to Florence. After marriage, Parthe changed; she grew calmer, more content.

Florence even attempted to repair her friendship with Marianne Nicholson, who was now married to a man named

"NO, MAMA, I SHALL NEVER FORGET IT."

Douglas Galton. The two had little left in common, but they remained on cordial and friendly terms. Douglas Galton was an engineer who was quite skilled at heating, ventilation, drains, and water supply. His expertise would prove to be quite valuable to Florence.

Thirty-six-year-old Florence Nightingale was now a famous woman. People wanted to meet her. She was inundated with invitations to dinners and receptions.

"Florence," her mother said, waving invitations she had rescued from the wastebasket. "What is the meaning of this? Have you responded to these invitations?"

"Yes, Mama," she replied. "I have indeed responded to them."

Fanny appeared relieved. "Then you must keep the invitations, dear, so that you remember the dates."

"That won't be necessary. I respectfully declined all of them."

Fanny Nightingale's mouth gaped. Knowing it was useless to argue, she shrugged and left the room. Her daughter had never been interested in being in the spotlight,

"I RESPECTFULLY DECLINED ALL OF THEM."

and Fanny supposed she wouldn't change now.

◆

Florence knew how poor her health had become. She sometimes feared she didn't have long to live.

"I'm afraid I will die before my work for You is completed," she prayed. "I ask for just enough time to complete the work I have started."

Florence was determined to change the army's medical practices. Fearing she had only a few years to do so, she went to work stirring up the country. She recounted horror stories of ill treatment the men had been given. She told of the sewer that ran under the hospital and other examples of the filth the soldiers had had to live with.

"And many men with open wounds were placed right next to men with cholera, pneumonia, and other infectious diseases. I separated them at Scutari, and fewer men died."

◆

Queen Victoria invited Florence to visit her at Balmoral Castle in Scotland. Over tea, the two women talked.

SHE SOMETIMES FEARED SHE DIDN'T HAVE LONG TO LIVE.

"Scutari touched my heart, Florence," Queen Victoria admitted. "Too many men died needlessly. I want you to tell me yourself what things were really like."

Queen Victoria had heard stories from news reporters, but preferred to hear things directly from Florence.

Florence told her of the dreadful things she had seen at Scutari.

"Improvements are desperately needed, Your Majesty," Florence pleaded. "Disease can be prevented in times of war and peace, but there have to be changes made in medical care and hospital living conditions."

"What changes do you suggest Florence?"

Florence hesitated. After all, she was speaking to the Queen of England.

"Please, Florence," the Queen continued. "I want your opinion because I trust your judgement. Don't be afraid to speak your mind."

"If you could set up a royal commission to evaluate existing medical services, it would help. If our soldiers are in better general health, I'm sure we would have fewer

SHE WAS SPEAKING TO THE QUEEN OF ENGLAND.

war casualties."

"What do you feel needs to change?"

"Cleanliness. Our hospitals must be clean, the patients themselves should be washed, and their clothing and bedding changed every day. Patients with contagious diseases should be separated from the wounded."

After hearing some of Florence's other suggestions, Queen Victoria agreed to consider them. After that visit, the two women became friends.

"What a head she has on her shoulders!" Queen Victoria told her ministers. "I am certainly glad she's on our side."

◆

A royal commission was formed. Florence, of course, would have been the best person to head such a commission. But women in those days, were not permitted to take such high offices.

"I wish I could change this silly tradition," the Queen sighed, but it was impossible.

Sidney Herbert was named head of the commission,

"WHAT A HEAD SHE HAS ON HER SHOULDERS!"

but Florence did most of the work. Florence uncovered problems and came up with solutions.

When the commission presented its reports, Florence's views of army hospitals became evident. Many of Florence's suggested changes were soon made.

With that accomplished, Florence was now free to turn her attention to her oldest dream—a school for training nurses.

The Nightingale Fund had grown to several hundred thousand dollars.

"That is more than enough to get us started," she said excitedly. "But where shall I have my school?"

Florence's school for nurses found a home at St. Thomas Hospital in London. It was a perfect setup. The nursing students could live at the hospital, and the doctors on staff would train them.

Things would never be the same for nurses or their patients. And all because God had called upon a young woman named Florence Nightingale.

The Nightingale School of Nursing opened on July 9,

ST. THOMAS HOSPITAL IN LONDON.

1860. This was an historic event. Until that time no one from the general public had been formally trained as a nurse. Only nuns or other religious women had been given formal training. Others were untrained women who were unable to work elsewhere.

Fifteen young women were carefully chosen to be the first class at the Nightingale School of Nursing.

"Standards for the Nightingale School are very high," Florence insisted. "My girls will come only from the best of families."

And rules were strict.

"There will be no drinking of spirits," Florence continued. "Gentleman callers will be allowed in the public only. No men will visit in the ladies' dormitories."

Despite Florence's success at Scutari, many people still thought little of nurses. They were believed to be uneducated drunkards unable to find other, more suitable employment.

"It is up to us, girls, to change that disgusting opinion. As the first class of the Nightingale School, you will be the

"IT IS UP TO US, GIRLS, TO CHANGE
THAT DISGUSTING OPINION."

pioneers. You will have to prove that nurses are capable of taking care of a patient's health and not just able to scrub floors. You must act and perform as professionally as any doctor. Only then will nurses gain the same respect as doctors.

Florence personally interviewed each applicant, and only with her approval were the women invited to attend the Nightingale School.

Florence kept close watch on her students, charting their progress during the yearlong training course.

The first class of the Nightingale School met with Florence at her home in London. They all looked like clones, dressed in plain brown dresses and starched white aprons. Their heads sported clean white caps that bobbed as the women excitedly chattered.

Florence herself had designed the uniforms. Until this time, nurses had worked in their everyday, sometimes dirty, clothing.

"Oh, Miss Nightingale, we can hardly wait to begin classes!"

"OH, MISS NIGHTINGALE, WE CAN
HARDLY WAIT TO BEGIN CLASSES!"

"And to work with the patients."

Florence smiled at their enthusiasm. "Ladies," she said, "I admire your eagerness, and I understand your impatience. But you have lots to learn before actually working with patients."

"But when will we work with patients on our own?"

"Not until the end of your training year."

A murmur of disappointment hummed around the room.

"You will work with patients, but under strict supervision." Florence went on to explain the daily routine of the Nightingale School. "You are required to be in the hospital wards by seven A.M. each morning. Anyone who is late without an acceptable excuse, will be severely reprimanded. Repeated tardiness will endanger your completing this nursing course."

Florence paused a moment to see if this had sunk in. Judging by the serious faces she saw, she assumed it had.

"The patients will be washed, fed, and given their medications. All that should keep you busy until lunchtime."

FLORENCE WENT ON TO EXPLAIN THE DAILY ROUTINE.

Florence went on to say that the afternoon would consist of a lecture given by one of the doctors on staff at St Thomas's Hospital.

"After the lecture, you will return to the wards and give patients their suppers. Your duties will be finished at 9:00 P.M., but that will not be the end of your day."

Florence watched eyes widen, and heard gasps. Now was the test. Anyone who could not stand the long hours would be weeded out early. Still, no one spoke up to object.

"You will neatly write up notes on the lecture, so that the head nurse and I can look them over." Florence paused and smiled. "That, then, will be the end of your long day. Does anyone have any questions?"

A delicate-looking young lady raised her hand. Florence nodded at her and she meekly asked, "When will we help the doctors in surgery?"

"You will have to sit through several lectures on treating different diseases before you'll be ready to assist the doctors in something as delicate as surgery."

"WHEN WILL WE HELP THE DOCTORS IN SURGERY?"

To these young nurse-hopefuls, their year-long training course seemed such a long time. But today's nurses have to attend college for at least four years, and sometimes five, to earn their nursing degrees.

This exciting time in Florence's life was marred by the death of her mentor, Sidney Herbert, on August 2, 1861.

That friendship had been one of the most valued of her life. She remained close friends with Sidney's wife, Liz

◆

Through all her years of experience, Florence Nightingale had become an expert on how to build and run hospitals. In 1859, she wrote a book called *Notes on Hospitals*; it was later updated and reissued in 1863.

Then, in 1860, she wrote *Notes on Nursing*. It was used by many nurses as a practical guidebook on nursing. Based on Florence's brilliant common sense, it stressed the importance of fresh air, cleanliness, and a balanced diet of healthy foods.

Notes on Nursing was an instant best-seller. It was

NOTES ON HOSPITALS AND NOTES ON NURSING.

practical and intelligent. Its sales were also based on the fact that Florence had become a popular public figure and women everywhere were anxious to hear everything she said. *Notes on Nursing* showed Florence at her best. It was witty and amusing, not somber and technical like some of her other writings. Later editions of *Notes on Nursing* included a section called "Minding Baby." This was added after Florence had done an in-depth study of diseases in maternity.

Notes on Nursing looked into a person's mental health, especially areas such as worries and loneliness, as well as physical health.

"Apprehension, uncertainty, waiting expectation, fear of surprise," Florence wrote, "do a patient more harm than any exertion. Remember, he is face to face with his enemy (disease) all the time, internally wrestling with him, having long imaginary conversations with him. You are thinking of something else." Florence Nightingale believed in treating a person's mental attitude as well as his physical body.

NOTES ON NURSING SHOWED FLORENCE AT HER BEST.

Notes on Nursing included helpful hints for nursing and hygiene in the home. The book was sold in the United States as well as England and was translated into many European languages.

Florence's book, *Notes on Hospitals,* was an expert treatise on how hospitals should be built and run. Florence was a consultant for many years in hospital construction and contributed to the design of several hospitals in England.

Fresh air and sunshine were still thought harmful, but Florence helped to overcome this notion. She recommended that hospitals be light and airy. She suggested pale pink walls instead of the standard dark, ugly green ones.

"Wards should have ample space between the beds," she stated. "Kitchens and laundry rooms should be clean and spacious."

Florence recommended glass or earthenware cups, hair mattresses, and iron bedsteads. These could be cleaned much easier than the tin cups and straw mattresses already in use.

SHE RECOMMENDED THAT HOSPITALS BE LIGHT AND AIRY.

But Florence didn't stop there! When a woman of God has it in her mind to do something, she will accomplish it.

She also studied drains, statistics, and new forms of record-keeping. Florence even came up with a new system for classifying diseases; she had been gifted with great knowledge and diligence.

HAD BEEN GIFTED WITH GREAT KNOWLEDGE AND DILIGENCE.

SHE HAD NOT BEEN TO LEA HURST SINCE 1856.

10
Independence

In October, 1865, William Nightingale bought Florence a house in a fashionable section of London. Her sunny bedroom overlooked a splendid cheerful garden. However, Florence lived only with her servants and, in spite of all her work, she was often lonely. She kept a number of cats who were permitted to roam the house at liberty. They often amused Florence in her bedroom with their antics. It was at this time that she began to study Greek again.

Florence's family persuaded her to visit them in the summer of 1868. She had not been to Lea Hurst since her return from Constantinople in 1856. Now forty-eight years old, she stayed with them for three months.

She then returned to London and tried to continue her work. But she was growing older and sickly. The last plans she'd made were for the foundations of the British Red Cross Aid Society in which she gave instructions on the care of the sick. She also helped raise money to aid victims of the Franco-Prussian War of 1870. But by 1872, she knew she had to slow down.

"I'm getting too old for this," she said to friends. "I can't keep up this pace anymore."

Remember, people weren't expected to live as long in the nineteenth century as they are now. Forty-eight or fifty might be considered middle-aged now, but in Florence's time, it was considered elderly. That her parents were still living at that time was quite unusual.

Florence wasn't the only one who was aging. Parthe was older than Florence. And William and Fanny Nightingale were quite advanced in years.

In 1872, William summoned Florence to Embley.

"Your mother and I are no longer able to manage our affairs," he informed her. "We need your help."

"I'M GETTING TOO OLD FOR THIS."

Because Parthe was married and Florence was not, William and Fanny felt it was Florence's place to help them. After all, they thought, Parthe had a husband to worry about; Florence had only those silly cats.

Florence hated the eight months she spent at Embley trying to sort out her parents' financial affairs. She couldn't wait to return to God's work, to her nursing school in London.

"The nurses are my closest friends," she confided to Parthe. "It is their gossip that keeps me up-to-date with the outside world."

Then, Florence and Aunt Mai had a falling out. Florence had fallen ill and Aunt Mai had chosen to tend to her own family instead of to Florence.

"They are bitter over being neglected so many times for you," Mia tried to explain as lovingly as possible. "And they are right. Much as I love you, dear Florence, I must think of my husband and children."

Florence's friend Hilary Bonham-Carter stayed with her in Hampstead until Mai returned in October, 1859.

FLORENCE HATED THE EIGHT MONTHS SHE SPENT AT EMBLEY.

But Mai realized she could no longer sacrifice her own family, and she left Florence again in 1860. Sadly, it would be twenty years before Florence could bring herself to speak to Aunt Mai again.

◆

William Edward Nightingale died on January 10, 1874. According to his will, Aunt Mai inherited most of the Nightingale fortune, including the estate at Embley.

"Please, Aunt Mai," Florence begged, "Mama and Papa spent most of their lives at Embley. Couldn't you let Mama stay until she dies?"

Mai, obviously hurt by Florence's anger at her, refused. By this time, Fanny Nightingale was blind and her mind was failing.

"Fine!" Florence said stubbornly. "Then I will care for her myself. She can live with me at my home."

Florence moved Fanny out of Embley in July, 1874. She cared for her until Fanny's death in 1880.

Uncle Sam, Mai's husband, died in 1881, and the two finally reconciled. Parthe fell ill shortly after that, and the

SHE CARED FOR HER UNTIL FANNY'S DEATH IN 1880.

sisters were close again until Parthe's death in 1890.

Florence seemed to return to her old self once the family wounds healed. She was even called back to work when the government asked her to look into the neglect of wounded soldiers in Egypt. That work, and some she later did in India, were the last official acts Florence Nightingale performed.

She was simply getting old. Even those called by God do not escape the aging process.

SHE WAS CALLED BACK TO WORK IN EGYPT.

YEARS OF OVERWORK HAD TAKEN THEIR TOLL ON HER BODY.

11
The Later Years

Aunt Mai carried in a tray of tea and lightly buttered toast. Florence frowned and shook her head. "Now, Florence," Aunt Mia scolded, "You must eat something. You have to keep up as much strength as possible."

Florence seldom left her London home, or her bed, now. Years of overwork had taken their toll on her body. She was now an invalid and ill most of the time. She had good friends and Aunt Mai to care for her.

Though Florence's body had weakened, the voice of God calling to her had not. She worked just as hard from her bed as she had before. The Nightingale School was quite successful, and Florence continued to guide it in spirit.

When Florence had lost the physical strength to run the Nightingale School, she entrusted it to her head nurse, Mrs. Wardroper.

Many women had completed courses at the Nightingale School of Nursing and were working in several countries. Some graduates went on to start nursing schools of their own. One of the graduates founded the first nursing school in the United States, at Bellevue Hospital in New York City.

"Your views on nursing have spread all over the world," Mai told Florence. "You are a worldwide heroine."

Florence waved away her praise. "I have only done what the Lord called me to do."

"Well," Aunt Mai went on, "it's not everyone who is called upon by the President of the United States."

The Civil War was raging in the United States, and President Lincoln's Secretary of War had remembered Florence's work in the Crimea. He asked Florence's advice.

"We need help setting up hospitals for the Union Army. And this is the first time our government has allowed

THE SECRETARY OF WAR REMEMBERED FLORENCE'S WORK.

women to nurse the soldiers. They need your practical advice, Miss Nightingale."

For the duration of the Civil War, Florence corresponded with Dorothea Dix, the Superintendent of Nurses in Washington, D.C. Because of the advice Florence had given, thousands of Union soldiers lived despite their wounds.

From her bed, Florence masterminded many critical reforms in medical care. She influenced many countries, not only her native England, concerning health care.

At that time, India was still a part of the British Empire—not the independent country it is today. Many English soldiers lived in India with their families.

India was not a terribly sanitary country then. Most people did not bathe or clean their teeth regularly.

"Their diet over there is atrocious!" Florence once exclaimed.

Illness ran rampant throughout India as a result of sanitation and diet. Many of the country's poor people died young.

"THEIR DIET OVER THERE IS ATROCIOUS!"

"India needs to improve its living conditions," Florence declared. "I suggest a royal commission be formed to study the case."

Florence worked behind the scenes, from her bed, to help India improve the life-style of its occupants. Following her suggestions, the British soldiers stationed there and the Indian people greatly improved their lives.

Florence was encouraged by the success in India. By 1888, there was a sanitary board in every province of the country.

In 1897, a grand celebration called the Diamond Jubilee marked Queen Victoria's sixtieth year of reign over England. There were many special programs to illustrate significant events that had happened during Victoria's reign. There was one exhibition on modern nursing.

"Praise Florence Nightingale, the pioneer of modern nursing!" hailed one member of the crowd.

"Long live the angel of Mercy!" cried another.

"The Lord's blessing to the Lady with the Lamp!"

Florence's popularity soared once again.

"THE LORD'S BLESSING TO THE LADY WITH THE LAMP!"

◆

During her final years, Florence was surrounded by the people she loved most. Close friends, her Aunt Mai, and Mai's youngest child, Shore, spent lots of time with her and cared for her when she was ill.

As she grew older, Florence gained weight and grew rather stout. Her eyes weakened, and she was totally blind by 1901. Florence took it as a sign from God.

"I have no choice but to slow down now," she told Shore. "But I have no regrets, my work here is done. Nurses are no longer scorned and hated, they are admired and revered for the important and difficult work they do."

As the new century dawned, Florence continued to receive public attention. In 1907, she was the first woman to receive Britain's Order of Merit Award.

"I can thank only God," Florence said, "for it was His call that led me to this work."

Henry Durant, founder of the International Red Cross, also paid tribute to Florence Nightingale. "It was Florence's brilliant work during the Crimean War that inspired me

"I HAVE NO REGRETS, MY WORK HERE IS DONE."

to found the International Red Cross," he said.

◆

Florence Nightingale never again left her bedroom after 1896. Still, in addition to receiving the Order of Merit Award, the Freedom of the City of London Award was conferred upon her in 1910.

Florence was much isolated for the last ten years of her life. She was blind and constantly ill. Most of her closest friends were dead, including Queen Victoria.

On August 13, 1910, the woman who had been called by God to do such important work, passed into His hands. Florence Nightingale was ninety years old.

Afterword

Reading a biography of Florence Nightingale is a study of opposites. All through her life, Florence suffered extremes; she either received extravagant praise for success, or extravagant blame for things gone wrong. She was seen as tenderhearted and sweet or as cold, ruthless, and quarrelsome.

Florence Nightingale is often portrayed as a rebel, someone determined to do the exact opposite of what her parents wished. But, as we can see, this was necessary for her to carry out the purpose the Lord had appointed her to.

"Since I was twenty-four," Florence once said, "there was never any vagueness in my plans or ideas as to what God's work was for me."

We must view Florence Nightingale, not as a rebel, but

as a strong woman determined to do God's will in the face of all resistance. In a letter to Florence, dated December 31, 1879, Benjamin Jowett, a professor at Oxford University, wrote:

> *There was a great deal of romantic feeling about you twenty-three years ago when you came home from the Crimea. And now you work on in silence, and nobody knows how many lives are saved by your nurses in hospitals; how many thousands of soldiers who would have fallen victims to bad air, bad drainage and ventilation, are now alive owing to your forethought and diligence; how many natives of India in this generation and in generations to come have been preserved from famine, oppression, and the load of debt by the energy of a sick lady who can scarcely rise from her bed. The world does not know all this, or think about it. But I know it, and often think about it. And I want you to think*

about it, so that in later years of your course you
may see what a blessed life yours is and has
been.

We can only imagine how much Florence appreciated
his letter. And how embarrassed she was by it. Florence
had spent her life hiding from the spotlight, undermining
her greatness, and scoffing at celebrity. She worked only
for God, and for the goodness of humankind, not for her
own glory.

Today, Florence Nightingale's portrait hangs in many
hospitals and nursing schools. Nursing hopefuls everywhere can pass under her likeness and look with rever-
ence and gratitude upon a great and grand lady who went
where God led her.

Bibliography

Colver, Anne, *Florence Nightingale, War Nurse*. Champaign, Ill.: Garrard Publishing, 1961.

Gibbs, Peter, *Crimean Blunder*. London: F. Muller, 1960

Harmelink, Barbara, *Florence Nightingale: Founder of Modern Nursing*. New York: Franklin Watts, Inc., 1969

Smith, F.B., *Florence Nightingale: Reputation and Power*. New York: St. Martin's Press, 1982.

Strachey, Lytton, *Eminent Victorians*. New York: Random House, 1918.

Woodham-Smith, Cecil, *Lonely Crusader: The Life of Florence Nightingale*. New York: Whittlesey House, 1951.